How To Quit Smoking

Without Giving Up Cigarettes

R.E. Barringham

Cheriton House Publishing

Published by Cheriton House Publishing - December 2009.

Republished 2019

Copyright © R.E. Barringham 2009
All rights reserved.

CiP data available Australian Libraries.
ISBN: 978-0-9803582-6-1

Important

No part of this publication may be reproduced, stored in or introduced into any retrieval system, or transmitted, in any form or by any means (including electronically, mechanically, recording, photocopying or otherwise) without the prior written permission of both the copyright holder (the author) and the publisher (Cheriton House Publishing) of this book.

It is illegal to scan, upload or distribute this book via the internet or via any other means without the permission of the publisher (Cheriton House Publishing) and doing so is punishable by law.

If you require an electronic version of this book, please only purchase authorized electronic editions and do not participate in, or encourage in any way, pirated copies of this book. Your support for this work and the author is very much appreciated.

Important Notice

All Information contained in this book is provided with the understanding that the author is not liable for any misconception, misuse or use of the information provided, nor is the author engaged in the practice of medicine, offering medical advice, or attempting to cure any disorders or diseases.

The author is simply providing information and leaves the final choice of what information the reader uses to the reader and the reader's health care provider.

The author shall have neither liability nor responsibility to any person or entity with respect to any loss, damage or injury caused or alleged to be caused directly or indirectly by the Information provided, or any use thereof.

You should seek the partnership of a qualified health care practitioner of your choice before using Information provided in this book.

If you have any special conditions requiring attention (medical, psychiatric or psychological), you are advised to consult with your health care practitioner regarding possible modifications of the information contained in this book.

The information provided in this book should not be construcd as personal medical advice or instruction. No action should be taken based solely on the information contained in this book.

Readers should always consult appropriate health professionals on any matter relating to their health and wellbeing.

The information and opinions provided in this book are believed to be accurate and sound, based on the best judgment available to the author, but readers who fail to consult appropriate medical or health advice from a qualified practitioner, assume the risk of any injuries, illness or disease resulting from the use of, or alleged to be resulting from the use of the information contained in this book.

Introduction

The Real Secret to Giving Up Smoking That No One Ever Wants to Talk About

Welcome to this brand new book "How to Stop Smoking Without Giving Up Cigarettes."

This book will introduce you to the best and easiest way to become a non-smoker.

You won't have to buy any expensive or useless products or use any sort of therapy and you won't have to quit smoking by going "cold turkey."

Instead, all you have to do is read this book, follow the simple step-by-step instructions and in a few months from now you'll not only be a non-smoker, but you'll wonder what on earth made you want to start smoking in the first place.

You see, when it comes to undoing the chains that bind you to your cigarettes, it seems hard to do because those chains aren't just an addiction, they're emotional chains that make you WANT to pick up a cigarette, light it, then sit back and enjoy inhaling and exhaling the smoke from your lungs.

The habit of smoking is so ingrained in your daily life that it seems that it actually is a part of your life.

So the only way to untie those smoking chains is link by link. This process won't be fast, but it doesn't want to be.

Learning to be a non-smoker will take you 8 to 9 months to accomplish using the methods in this book. But you will be gently guided all the way with new methods to incorporate into your life each month until eventually, you'll be able to look behind you and see that the chains you thought were binding you have finally fallen away.

But how are you going to quit smoking without giving up cigarettes; because if you're still smoking, you can't be quitting. Right?

Wrong.

I'll explain the whole process soon. But first I want to tell you the real secret to giving up smoking that no one ever wants to talk about.

The Real Secret

When it comes to giving up smoking you can find any number of products aimed at helping you to quit. Now I'm not going to tell you that those products aren't any good. Some of them are probably excellent at what they do and no doubt serve their purpose. But there is a secret to giving up smoking, and without it nothing in the whole world will make you stop smoking.

And the secret is simple.

You have to WANT to be a non-smoker.

AND...

You MUST feel happy about it.

As a human you're always ruled by your emotions. So no matter what you're doing, every action you take is fueled by an emotion. And it doesn't matter if it's a good emotion or a bad emotion. It will still be having an effect on everything you do.

If you're doing something that makes you unhappy or anxious, then your enthusiasm and success will be low or non-existent. But if you're doing something, or thinking about doing something, that makes you happy, then you'll feel motivated and energetic about doing it.

So when it comes to quitting cigarettes you have to stay focused on your goal and not on the process of getting there. And your goal MUST be to become a non-smoker. Your goal must NOT be to give up cigarettes.

Why?

Because if you want to become a non-smoker you SHOULDN'T want to quit smoking. In fact you shouldn't even be THINKING about giving up smoking, because using the words 'quitting' or 'giving up' are negative words and so they make you feel bad. If you think about 'giving up' and 'quitting' all the time, you'll instantly feel defeated because in your subconscious mind you'll feel as though you will be missing out on something if you stop smoking.

We usually use the term 'giving up' when we fail to do something, like when you work at a task and keep failing and so eventually you throw your hands in the air and say "I Give Up!" and walk away and leave the task unfinished.

And if you hate your job and the boss gets on your back about something you shout "I Quit!" and walk out.

Both these expressions have negative associations so it's no surprise that when applied to smoking they can cause you to become anxious.

And maybe, just maybe, you WANT to feel anxious about not smoking so that when you fail to stop smoking you feel less guilty about it. This also helps you to associate smoking with happy feelings which is not helpful if you're trying to stop.

And feeling happy about smoking, even though you SAY you want to stop, will only facilitate in making you think that you CAN'T stop smoking.

So instead of trying to find ways to stop smoking, you'll run around wasting your time looking for a magic pill that will make you WANT to stop. And sadly, there is no such thing.

The whole sad truth of the matter is that if you don't really feel that you want to stop smoking, then you never will.

There's an old saying that whether you think you can or you think you can't, you're right.

So you have to WANT to be a non-smoker. You have to feel joyful at the thought of finally living your life free of cigarettes.

You have to close your eyes and see yourself as a non-smoker. You have to think about drinking a cup of tea or coffee without having a cigarette in your other hand at the same time – AND – this thought has to make you feel great.

You have to be able to imagine yourself leaving the house every day WITHOUT your cigarettes and you must feel cheerful about it. At the moment the thought of going anywhere without a large supply of cigarettes will probably make you shiver. But when you can REALLY see yourself as a non-smoker AND the thought makes you feel good, then you WILL be able to stop smoking.

And if it doesn't? Just close this book now, light up your next cigarette and admit to yourself that you really don't want to stop smoking at all.

Do you?

How to Quit Without Giving Up

If you're still reading and you haven't closed this book, as previously suggested, then you really do want to quit smoking and the thought of becoming a non-smoker fills you with so much joy that you're 100% motivated about reaching your goal.

Great!

So now you need to know how you're going to do it. So let's begin...

When it comes to smoking, most people automatically associate quitting with instantly giving up cigarettes.

But you don't start smoking by suddenly smoking a pack or more a day, so you shouldn't give up by suddenly NOT smoking a pack or more every day.

Becoming a smoker takes time. You begin by smoking one or two cigarettes a day, and gradually increase it over a period of time until you're smoking 20 or more a day. But it's not easy going from 20 or more cigarettes a day to zero. Or I should correctly say, it's not easy going from 20 or more cigarettes a day to zero if you're trying to do it in one split second. Is it really possible to be a smoker one minute and a non-smoker the next?

It's much easier to stop smoking the same way you began, and that means stopping slowly until you feel that you no longer want to smoke. That way you won't be 'giving up' anything. Instead you'll be putting an end to a bad habit that no longer holds any interest for you.

The only reason that smoking cigarettes holds any interest for you now, is because you don't know how to leave them alone.

Most smokers try and give up by going 'cold turkey' but this method rarely works because rather than becoming an instant non-smoker, all you become is a smoker without any cigarettes.

The reason that trying to quit smoking instantly is referred to as going 'cold turkey' is because 'cold turkey' is an expression used to explain how drug addicts suffer when they try and 'kick the habit' of taking drugs.

When they instantly stop using drugs, they go through a phase called 'cold turkey'. This is because one of the first symptoms the addict feels is uncontrollable shivering and their skin becomes like turkey flesh (i. e. goose bumps) which can last for several days or several weeks.

After this phase has passed the addict then suffers uncontrollable leg spasms which is where the phrase 'kicking the habit' comes from.

Going through all this physical suffering is very difficult for any drug addict because they know that simply using the drugs again will put an end to their suffering.

Smokers, on the other hand, suffer much less when giving up their addiction because the only withdrawal symptom is the desire to smoke. So when you compare that to what the drug addicts suffer, giving up cigarettes SHOULD be easy.

But it isn't.

My Story

I used to be a smoker myself and smoked 20 to 25 cigarettes a day. I often thought about giving up but I wasn't really sure how to do it.

At first I tried hypnotherapy. I found the whole experience very relaxing and great for stress relief. I would lay on my bed every day and listen to my hypnotherapy tapes. But as soon as I sat up, I'd instantly feel like smoking a cigarette.

At the same time I also knew another person who was trying to stop smoking. She too tried hypnotherapy. She also read several books and tried several different courses. But to this day she still smokes.

I realized after watching her for several years that her problem wasn't in the treatments and books she was using. Her failure was in the fact that she really didn't want to stop smoking and instead was looking for that magic 'something' that would make her WANT to stop. She just couldn't see that unless she herself wanted to stop, nothing was going to make it happen. She simply could never see herself as a non-smoker.

I too had looked into several different ways of giving up smoking while I continued to smoke.

Then my awakening moment came one stormy night in 1990.

It was about 6pm and my 6-year-old son and I had just finished dinner. Outside there was quite a storm raging. I had run out of cigarettes that afternoon and because of the bad weather, I tried to convince myself that I would be fine without a cigarette for the rest of the day.

But once our evening meal was finished I was "DYING" for a cigarette. But I didn't have any, so I washed the dishes and told myself that I'd be fine.

Then about half an hour later I was thinking of getting my son ready for bed. But the thought of sitting on my own all evening without any cigarettes was worrying.

There was a petrol station about 5 minutes' walk from our house so I decided to risk it and walk there (I didn't have a car). After all, how wet could we get in such a short space of time? It was also a cold night so I dressed my young son and myself in our warmest coats and hats and put on our wellington boots.

Then we set off out the front door to get my cigarettes. We walked as fast as we could but the water was gushing down the road and over our feet and the rain really lashed our faces.

By the time we got home again we were soaked. We took off our hats and coats and hung them to dry. The rain was so heavy that it had penetrated our clothes too and our hair was plastered to our heads.

We stripped off our clothes and I started to towel my son's hair. I saw for the first time how cold and wet he was and as I watched him shiver I burst into tears. How could I have been so selfish to drag the poor little boy out in such bad weather for something as unimportant as cigarettes?

I don't need to tell you that I didn't enjoy smoking the cigarettes that night. Every time I looked at the packet I was reminded of how self-seeking I'd been and I felt miserable that my need for cigarettes had been more important to me than my son's well-being.

I knew at that moment that I no longer wanted to smoke. I knew that if I was a non-smoker I'd never drag my son out in a storm ever again AND we'd have more money to spend if I wasn't wasting it all on cigarettes. I felt like a totally selfish mother and I was determined to do something about it.

So although I was feeling bad about what I'd done, I also felt elated because I knew that I was going to stop smoking. And I did.

I didn't do it instantly. Instead I used a slow system of quitting so that gradually, over the next few months, I smoked less and less, till eventually I wasn't smoking at all.

Other smokers that I knew were amazed how I cut smoking out of my life for good and they began to ask me the exact method I'd used.

So I began to help them all, taking them step-by-step and month-by-month through how I did it and they did it too.

Eventually I began helping more and more people to stop smoking and now I have decided to put my complete method in a book so that anyone can do it.

Becoming a non-smoker isn't easy, but it's not impossible. I know, because when I started to

become a non-smoker, although I was determined to do it, I still found it hard.

But my slow and steady system for getting cigarettes out of your life for good makes the whole process easy. In fact, you'll hardly even notice that you're stopping.

All you have to do is work your way through this book and follow ALL the advice given. Then in 9 months' time you'll be a non-smoker.

Can you imagine how fantastic that is going to be?

No more buying expensive cigarettes.

No more worrying about your health.

No more smelling like a dirty ashtray.

And most of all, no more cigarettes dominating your life.

By the end of this book you will be free of cigarettes forever.

Chapter 1

Why Do People Start Smoking?

When people first start smoking they do it for many different reasons, but they don't always realize that the first cigarette that they 'try' when they are younger, could develop into a habit that they cannot control.

A lot of the time, people try their first cigarette because of peer pressure. There was a good example of this happening in the movie *Grease* when Olivia Newton-John (Sandy) was pressured by her school friends to take a puff of a cigarette during a sleep-over at her cousin's house. She clearly didn't want to, but the constant goading of the other girls left her with no option because she was, at that time, trying to 'fit in' at her new school.

When we're young, peer pressure, and the fear of not 'fitting in' can have a huge influence on our behavior. There are very few children who finish school without at least once trying to smoke a cigarette. This is because while we're at school, the opinion of our fellow students can seem more important than the opinions of our parents; or our own common sense.

But smoking doesn't always start because of peer pressure. Sometimes children are just curious and want to try something just to see what it's like, especially if they constantly see adults doing it. Just as children like to try a sip of alcohol when they're younger, they want to try cigarettes. Adults don't always see anything wrong with allowing a child to take a sip of their drink, but they usually draw the line at letting them take a puff of their cigarette.

So instead children will turn to other kids to experiment with smoking.

Some so-called 'tougher' children want to start smoking cigarettes because they think it makes them look 'cool'. And although they might be admired for it (or not) by their friends, when adults see a child with a cigarette it just looks silly.

But that is exactly what smoking is. It's silly. There is no need to do it, there is nothing good or advantageous about it, it costs a lot of money and is bad for our health and our environment.

Yet even knowing this when we are children it still didn't stop us from wanting to try it.

Then as we get older it sometimes seems sophisticated to smoke. A young 20-something may feel more 'grown up' with a smoking cigarette held between their fingers. Why?

Because in a young mind, smoking is still seen as 'grown up'. 20-somethings often feel as though they are still treated as children by older people and so will often use cigarettes to try and make themselves appear older, more sophisticated or more mature.

Smoking is also used by the young as an act of defiance. No parent wants their off-spring to start smoking at a young age, and kids know this. So they use smoking to gain what they see as control of part of their life. Children are told what to do on a daily basis and can sometimes feel as though their lives are completely controlled by their parents, teachers and carers, and so smoking without permission gives them a feeling of control.

A big 'show off' factor can also be a part of it as children rarely smoke alone. They either want the whole world to see (except their parents and teachers) or they want their friends to see. But either way, they want to show off and say "Hey, look what I can do and no one can stop me."

Children can also feel that smoking makes them 'individual' even though thousands of people all over the world are doing the same thing.

Where I live there are a bunch of teenagers who hang out in the city center every single day and wear "Goth" clothes and make-up so they have black everything including clothes, hair, make-up and nails. And the reason they do it, when asked, is that they are simply being individual. How that works I have still yet to discover but it seems to make them think they are different from everyone else even though there are so many of them all hanging out in the same place and all looking the same.

Likewise children who smoke will all congregate together to smoke and to discuss how different they are to everyone else. This can, for all the wrong reasons, supply a secure feeling of 'belonging'. And when something makes you feel good, you always want to continue doing it.

On the other hand some children will smoke to prove that they do not belong to anyone. These are the children who are constantly truant from school and hang out all on their own. They swear that they are different from all the other kids because they don't take any sh*t from anyone and prove their complete defiance and disregard for rules by smoking, whether they enjoy it or not, and usually, they don't enjoy it at all.

Sadly a child who stays away from other children and smokes is usually mistaking the cigarettes for comfort. They feel secure when they have a packet of cigarettes in their pocket as though they are carrying a friend with them.

This situation can also apply to some adults. Some people actually feel comforted by knowing that they have their cigarettes with them. People who live alone will sit down to watch TV in the evenings with a cup of tea or coffee in one hand and a cigarette in the other. And when they're not smoking they will still sit with the cigarette packet on the arm of the sofa or on the coffee table because they somehow feel less lonely if they have their cigarettes close by.

Boredom can also be a reason to smoke. It's all too easy to think "I'll just sit down and have a cigarette. " But what you're actually doing is looking for an excuse to do nothing, instead of doing what you should be doing. And this can be a bad habit to get into, not only because it makes you lazy, but because the cigarettes are slowly killing you.

It's also all too easy to believe that smoking makes you happy. I've met countless people who have told me that they absolutely love to smoke. They say it gives them so much pleasure that they cannot imagine their life without their cigarettes.

But when you start asking more questions, it soon becomes obvious that they don't actually enjoy smoking at all. No one does. It's just that they can't stop and so they try and convince themselves that they love to smoke. When asked about the health issue they'll even say that they don't care about their health and will come out with statements like "Well I might get run over by a bus so I may as well enjoy my life while I can" or "I'd rather have a short and happy life than a long and miserable one and smoking makes me happy so I don't mind dying young. "

I always ask them, that if smoking is so enjoyable, then why don't they just sit and smoke instead of distracting themselves by watching TV or reading a magazine, and they always say that watching TV or reading helps them to enjoy the cigarette rather than distracting them from it. But when you watch someone smoking, they never seem to be enjoying it. Instead they look exactly like what they are; and that is, someone who doesn't know how to stop smoking.

Years ago, advertisements for cigarettes were a problem. All those classy ads made cigarettes seem like pure pleasure waiting to be had. They even photographed the cigarette packets in exotic locations or in wealthy surroundings to make them look even more appealing.

And then cigarette companies became big sponsors of sport and so their brand name and logos appeared on TV screens and billboards regularly.

These ads only encouraged people to see smoking as a normal way of life. It also didn't help that a lot of television shows depicted people smoking. The best known example of this was the TV detective series 'Colombo'. In every show Lieutenant Colombo was seen constantly smoking a cigar – even at the crime scenes! And the children's series of 'Batman' from the 1960s always showed The Penguin dressed in a tuxedo and smoking a cigarette through a long cigarette holder.

All these things made smoking appear as a normal part of life and had an unconscious influence on people's smoking habits. But thankfully, in a lot of countries, cigarette advertising has been banned and television shows no longer show the main characters as heavy smokers. Also many public places, buses, trains, shops, offices, bars and restaurants, no longer allow smoking. So now it's not as common to see people smoking and so it is no longer 'the norm' in most people's lives.

And this is a good thing because smoking shouldn't be seen as being a normal part of our everyday life. Children are always being influenced by what they see around them, whether it's something good or something bad.

A child that constantly sees their parents arguing will grow up to think that heated arguments are a normal part of marriage. A child who constantly sees his parents drinking alcohol every day will grow up thinking that drinking alcohol is a normal part of a daily routine. And likewise, a child who sees their parents smoking 20 times a day, every day, will grow up with an unconscious belief that smoking is simply just part of being an adult. And as discussed earlier, a child who associates smoking with adulthood will want to take up smoking as soon as possible to prove that they are no longer a child.

It's difficult enough for a child to grow into a balanced adult. But they shouldn't be unduly influenced to adopting bad habits along the way. It doesn't matter if it's smoking, drinking, drugs, gambling or over-eating. A child should not be subjected to bad habits that eventually become their ordinary way of life and cause them suffering.

So just as the blatant advertising of cigarettes has been taken out of the adult media, so too should they be kept out of a child's life. If a child wants to take up bad habits when they are older, it should be their choice to do so and not because it's a result of life-long conditioning.

You see, when people smoke cigarettes, they feel as though smoking is part of who they are rather than just a habit that they can't or won't break. This is doubly enforced when filling out medical forms that include the question "Are you a smoker?" Because this is how people start to view themselves and they reinforce it with statements such as "I've been a smoker for most of my life".

Statements such as these make those who smoke seem as though they belong to a particular group of humans. They see all human life as divided into two groups – the smokers and the non-smokers. And strangely enough they see 'the smokers' as a socially elite group of people and tend to figuratively 'look down' on those who are non-smokers.

Yet at the same time, those who don't smoke look upon those who do smoke as having a 'dirty' habit.

So if you smoke, and you truly want to quit, you need to stop seeing yourself as a 'smoker'. You are not a smoker. A chimney is a smoker. You are merely a person who inhales smoke from cigarettes. So disconnect yourself mentally from those who smoke. It is not a group to whom you really want to belong.

The problem though, with thinking of yourself as being a non-smoker, is that smoking cigarettes is seen as a way of life. A person who smokes is someone who hangs out with others who smoke during breaks at work, who sits in the smoking areas, who shops at the cigarette stores and collects cute ashtrays. And funnily enough, it's probably difficult for you to imagine your house without ashtrays.

It's so easy to associate smoking with how you live your life. Smoking isn't just what you do it's who you are. Just like people who stand up in AA meetings and announce that they are an alcoholic, you tell people that you are a smoker.

Are you proud of the fact that you smoke? Well, that probably depends on who you're talking to, or the group of humans they belong to – the smokers or the non-smokers. When you're with others who smoke it's easy to discuss your favorite brand of cigarettes, or how you burned a cigarette hole in your favorite shirt or the new cigarette lighter you bought.

But when you're in the company of those who don't smoke, you find it better not to talk about smoking at all because they won't find any of your smoking related topics worth listening to, and they may even start asking awkward questions like asking why you smoke.

And it's because you see the world as being divided into two groups, smokers and non-smokers, that makes giving up smoking seem like more of a life-changing situation rather than just a habit you want to break. Because once you give up the cigarettes for good, you'll be one of THOSE people – a non-smoker.

And you wouldn't be wrong in thinking that this will change your life in quite a few ways. At first it will seem strange at work when all the smokers leave the room at break time and go and smoke cigarettes without you. And it will seem strange to be with your friends who still smoke and see them passing around cigarettes and not offering you one.

Can you handle changes in your life like these?

Of course you can, because you're looking forward to becoming a non-smoker.

And what is a non-smoker? A happy person who has more money and better health because, unlike the people who smoke, a non-smoker is not burdened by the insistent and unwanted compulsion to light up cigarettes and suck the smoke into their lungs.

Just imagine how great it's going to be to feel so free.

Chapter 2

Why Smokers Don't Want to Stop Smoking

Ask anyone who smokes if they want to stop doing it and they'll say no.

Ask them why they don't want to stop and they'll give any one of the following reasons:

Why should I?
I don't want to.
I enjoy it.
It's my own little reward.
It's what I've always done.
It relaxes me.
It's not hurting anyone.
Life's too short to stop. May as well enjoy it while I can.

There are also quite a few other reasons that they'll give you but they will all become very insistent that they love to smoke.

Are you just like them?

If you smoke, you HAVE to always say that you enjoy smoking or else you'd appear stupid for doing it. Yet the chances are that most of the time you wish you didn't have to smoke. But the habit is too strong and too ingrained into your daily routine for you to be able to stop.

And it's just the same with an alcoholic wanting another drink. They will say that they want to drink because they enjoy it. But in reality, they just don't know how to stop.

And so it is with smokers. You don't really want to smoke. You just don't know how to get out of the habit of lighting up.

And you'll notice that there are certain times in the day, and certain circumstances, when you feel you absolutely must smoke a cigarette, such as after a meal or during a work break.

Why?

Because these are the times that you habitually smoke. Some people, while still eating a meal, are already thinking of the cigarette they will be lighting up afterwards. THAT'S how ingrained this habit can become. You can't enjoy a meal if you can't have a cigarette afterwards. Or you can't enjoy a drink unless you have a cigarette in your other hand.

Or you can't drink a cup of tea or coffee unless you're smoking a cigarette at the same time.

And it's these times of routinely smoking that cause you to become addicted to cigarettes.

It has very little to do with the actual nicotine addiction. Instead it's all about the habit you have of smoking a cigarette at a certain time or in a particular place.

For instance. I used to have a friend who not only was a non-smoker, but was strongly opposed to anyone smoking near her or in her house. I knew her during the 20 or so years that I smoked but whenever I went to her house I never took my cigarettes with me.

And you know what? Whenever I was at her house, I never even thought about smoking. But as soon as I left, I was dying for a cigarette.

It was obvious that my lack of desire for a cigarette at her house was just a non-smoking habit that I had gotten into. My mind just didn't associate her house with smoking, and so I never wanted to smoke when I was there. Also her house smelled very fresh because she kept it spotlessly clean and no one in her family smoked. So not only could I not smoke there but there were also no smells in her house associated with smoking.

And it's the same if you go to see the doctor or dentist. You can sit in the waiting room for ages without a cigarette, and because you know you can't smoke there, your desire to so is diminished.

This same habit of smoking applies to any particular time or place where you usually do or don't smoke. If it's a place or a time when you don't smoke then you probably never will. But if there is a time or a place where you do usually smoke, then you'll always want to.

Say for instance that every time you leave your house you light up a cigarette. It will become such an ingrained habit that every time you leave your house you'll automatically feel as if you HAVE to light a cigarette.

And because you feel that you HAVE to smoke at these certain times you will convince yourself that you actually enjoy smoking. When the truth really is that smoking is a habit that you find very difficult to break, even the small habit of lighting up a cigarette every time you leave your house.

But if you told yourself the truth about the situation, the truth being that you feel that you have no choice whether or not to smoke at certain times, then you'd have to admit that you have an addiction.

But it's not just the habit of smoking that keeps those cigarettes glowing.

There is also the problem of laziness. Smoking quickly becomes a lazy habit because it's much easier to just keep smoking rather than try and stop.

Some people even say that smoking puts them in their "comfort zone. " But a comfort zone is what we used to call a rut. We just say comfort zone instead so that it becomes an acceptable standard of living.

If you admit that you're in a rut, even a smoking rut, then you have no excuse for staying there. No excuse, that is, except laziness.

Giving up cigarettes, just like giving up any bad habit, takes effort. This can be minimal effort or maximum effort, depending on which frame of mind you are in. But either way it will take effort.

Even using the method outlined in this book, although it's easy to do, it will require a small amount of effort to actually read the book and follow the advice. This is minimal effort but some would rather stay in their comfort zone, or rut, rather than use minimal effort to improve their life. And because you're reading this book, I know you are not one of them.

The real problem with giving up smoking is that most people wouldn't even know where to start, let alone how to continue. So they usually try the only way they can think of, and that is to go "cold turkey. " I've even seen well-meaning ads on the television that tell people to decide on a day to quit smoking and then stop. But if it was really that easy, then everyone would be giving up that way. But choosing a day to quit, all that achieves is to make you dread that day arriving.

My advice is to not even try it. I've known people that have stopped smoking that way and it's worked for months or even years. But eventually they admit that all they've ever done since that day is wish they had a cigarette. So in the end they always go back to smoking again.

But no one is really sure of any other way to give up. So some people will start buying nicotine patches and sticking them all over their arms and legs. But this doesn't work either because it's not the nicotine addiction that's the real problem. It's the actual habit of holding a cigarette between your fingers and smoking it that's hard to break.

And all the time you're trying different ways to stop smoking, you get pressure from other smokers to give up giving up. They'll even try and force you to carry on smoking by offering you cigarettes all the time and taunting you by being negative and saying that you'll never do it; that you'll never give up.

And the problem is that they're right because you're thinking the same thing. You stand around with others who smoke and think to yourself that you really want to be smoking too. So when they say that you'll never give up, they are only confirming the thoughts that are already in your own mind.

And while you're going through the process of cutting cigarettes out of your life and wondering if you will make it, you are also haunted with the fear that you will no longer 'fit in' with your smoking friends because you don't need to go outside with them for a cigarette any more.

But the truth is that if you really have the desire to stop smoking for good, and you have the determination to do it, then you won't even care about whether or not you will 'fit in' with those who smoke. It will never be an issue unless you want to make it one.

Smokers always feel different to non-smokers. But non-smokers aren't really interested in whether someone they work with, or one of their friends, smokes or not.

I once knew a woman who was a heavy smoker and whenever she came to my house we would sit and smoke lots of cigarettes together. When I stopped smoking she would still come to my house just as often and the only difference was that she would smoke and I wouldn't. But because I wasn't smoking with her, she smoked much less.

And because I was no longer addicted to smoking, I felt sorry for her because she was still trapped in the habit. It felt good to sit and drink tea or coffee and not have to light up a cigarette at the same time as she still had to do. She even said to me one night that she envied me because of that and said that she wished she knew how to drink a cup of coffee without a cigarette.

And yet, even though she longed to stop smoking and had tried lots of different ways to quit, if I even lightly mentioned that she should stop smoking, she would get very angry and defensive about it.

But that is always the reaction of people who smoke. If you ask them why they don't quit, they become angry and will probably tell you that it's none of your business.

Is that what you do?

People always come out fighting when backed into a corner. And asking a smoker why they don't stop smoking makes them feel cornered because they don't have a rational reason to smoke and, what's even more frustrating for them is that they don't have a rational reason why they don't stop.

But ultimately no one wants to fail at anything and so sometimes smokers don't want to quit because they fear failure. They don't want to go around telling everyone that they're going to stop smoking and then admit to failure when it doesn't happen.

And giving up smoking isn't something that can be done privately. As soon as you aren't seen with a lit cigarette between your fingers during your usual smoking times, people will start to ask why.

So if you want to quit smoking you'll have to publicly admit what you're doing because you won't be able to hide it. But as I've said before, if you're determined and motivated to quit, then failure won't be a possibility, so you'll have nothing to fear.

The Law of Attraction is a belief that our lives depend on our thoughts, so whatever you think about the most is what you receive. So if you're trying to give up smoking and you keep thinking "I don't want to fail. I don't want to fail," *The Law of Attraction* states that it doesn't matter if you're thinking about failing or thinking about NOT failing; if you're thinking about failing in any way then you'll fail.

Likewise, if you're thinking "I'm going to give up smoking. I'm going to give up smoking," you're still thinking about smoking and so that is what you'll continue to do.

Instead you should be thinking "I'm a non-smoker. I'm a non-smoker," so that is what you'll become.

On the flip side of the fear of failing to stop smoking, there are others who won't try and quit because they're afraid they'll succeed.

Quite often people won't try something new, even if it's something that they really want to do, because they're afraid of succeeding.

But it's not because they don't want to succeed, but because they're afraid of the changes in their life that their success will bring.

For instance, some people dream of running their own business, but they never do it because they're afraid that it will change their life too much if they quit the job they've had for years and have to start a business from scratch.

Others dream of writing a best-selling novel. Yet despite their strong desire to do it and their considerable writing talent, they continue to resist writing. And it's not the fear of failure that holds them back but their fear of how different their life would be as a successful author.

Likewise smokers resist their urge to quit because they fear they might succeed and the thought of the changes that it will bring to their lives is greater than their desire to stop.

Are you one of these people? Have you tried different ways to quit in the secret hope that you won't succeed?

If that sounds like you then you must stop letting the fear of success hold you back from reading this book and following all the advice. Because if your desire to stop smoking is strong then the methods in this book WILL help you to stop smoking for good.

But as I've said before, becoming a non-smoker has to be your ultimate goal and you mustn't be afraid of succeeding, otherwise you'll allow resistance to thwart your efforts.

But as any dedicated smoker knows, giving up smoking isn't just a physical process. Smokers always take their cigarettes with them everywhere they go so there is a lot of emotion involved between a smoker and their cigarettes.

To become a regular smoker in the first place, you have to convince yourself that you "love" to smoke. But no one takes up smoking because they "love" to do it. As previously discussed you probably started smoking when you were younger for many different reasons. But none of those reasons still apply. So now it's time to stop.

But the problem is that for years your cigarettes have been your constant companion. And even when you've been on your own and felt as though others had let you down, your cigarettes were still there with you.

And whenever you felt lonely, anxious, depressed or otherwise miserable, you could always smoke a cigarette to help you feel better.

But the sad hard truth is that cigarettes are not your best friend, despite the way it feels to the contrary sometimes. So you have to accept that your cigarettes have never "loved" you back and you need to unravel yourself from the emotional bonds that binds you to your cigarettes.

Once you're sure that the emotional ties can be undone and your desire to be a non-smoker is the biggest and most important goal right now, then it's time to start your journey of a life without cigarettes.

But because the journey is emotional as well as physical you have to have a clear mental image of your future life as a non-smoker.

Right now it may be difficult to imagine your life without cigarettes, but it's something that you MUST do; and you must do it every day to keep your "eye on the prize."

You see, it's all too easy to get so caught up in the process of something that you forget what your ultimate goal is and how great it will be once you finally achieve it.

Take overweight people for example. They decide to lose weight. At first they're excited at the thought of being 20/50/100 kilos lighter. They may even begin their weight-loss regime gleefully with high hopes and great expectations. But as soon as they discover that their weight's not going down as fast as they wanted and they're missing their favorite foods, they get so caught up in the depravation they feel they're suffering that they can only see bleak days ahead of being denied the food they want. This makes them forget their goal of being slim and healthy as they continue to wallow in what they see as the sad and difficult process of dieting.

And the same thing can happen to you if you let it. You can get so caught up with the process of becoming a non-smoker that you can forget why you're doing it.

Instead you need to have an ultimately clear goal in mind of not only being a non-smoker, but of what you'll be doing instead. Smoking takes up a lot of time. If it only takes 5 minutes to smoke a cigarette and you smoke 20 cigarettes a day, that's over one and a half hours a day spent smoking. And as everyone knows, if you give up one thing, you have to replace it with another.

When athletes retire they become coaches or personal trainers. When overweight people stop overeating they start exercise routines or join a gym. When drug addicts give up drugs they become drug councilors or train for some other job. When alcoholics give up drinking they get a whole new life.

I once knew a man who was an alcoholic. Despite being married and having two children he just wouldn't stop drinking. Then one day he became very ill. He felt so bad that he thought he was dying. His doctor told him his condition was alcohol-related and that if he didn't stop drinking he would die.

This man was so shocked at how close he'd come to death (he was only 30 years old at the time) that he stopped drinking immediately (except for the odd bottle of wine at dinner with his wife, etc).

A year later I saw him and his wife. He looked really well. His wife looked great too and they'd had another child. They had also bought a new house, a new car, opened their own business (which was thriving) and they were enjoying life immensely. His wife said she'd never realised how much time and money he was wasting on drinking until he stopped.

And you will also find that you'll have much more time and money once you stop smoking. Not only that, but you'll be free of other restrictions too.

You see, another problem with smoking is that you're obliged to do it whether you want to or not. You can't just wake up in the morning and think "I'm not going to smoke any cigarettes today," or "I'm a bit short of money so I won't buy any cigarettes this week. " If you smoke you don't have choices when it comes to cigarettes. You HAVE to buy them and you HAVE to smoke them.

This limits your life to only being able to sit or stand in designated smoking areas in restaurants, cinemas, etc, not being able to smoke in non-smokers homes, having to go outside to smoke during coffee breaks at work and generally being forced outside in all weathers to smoke your cigarettes because many public (and private) places no longer allow smoking.

But once you become a non-smoker none of these restrictions will apply. You can go anywhere you want for as long as you want without having to worry about where the smoking areas are located or how long you're going to have to go without a cigarette while you're in the non-smoking areas.

You'll have more time, more money and no smoking-related worries. You'll finally be free to enjoy a meal, a drink or a cup of tea or coffee without the unwelcome urge to light up a cigarette every time.

Being free of cigarettes forever is the goal that you must always keep in mind and continually strive for without getting caught up in thinking about the process of getting there.

Reading this book and following all the steps in it is all you need. So forget about how you're going to achieve your goal and just trust in the methods within these pages to do it for you.

And don't think that becoming a non-smoker will change you. You won't change from the person you are just because you stop smoking cigarettes.

People who smoke always think about smoking. They think about it every day. As soon as they put out one cigarette, they instantly think about when their next one will be. Smoking seems as though it's not just a habit, it's a way of life.

But it isn't. Life without cigarettes isn't very different, but it is better and far cheaper. Smoking is expensive not only because of the actually cost of buying cigarettes, but because you also have to buy matches/lighters and ashtrays. Then there is the damage the smoke does to your home such as nicotine stained ceilings and walls that need redecorating, and your furniture needs washing often to get the smell of the smoke out, and even then you can't get rid of all the bad smell.

But once you no longer smoke, you and your home and your car will look and smell cleaner. You'll also have more free time and you'll feel better. Your life without your cigarettes won't be different; it will just be much, much better.

And don't worry about gaining weight. Many people who want to stop smoking worry that they'll eat more.

But this book won't let you do that. Using the information that you're about to learn will help you to make sure you don't replace smoking with eating.

There are very few people who gain weight when they stop smoking. And the ones who do, are just using giving up smoking as a poor excuse to overeat.

There is simply no reason to replace cigarettes with food, as you will discover. Eating food instead of smoking a cigarette will not make you feel better. In fact it will make you feel bad. And that bad feeling will make you go back to smoking again because you'll feel less guilty about smoking than you do about overeating.

But smoking and eating have nothing in common with each other so one cannot be used to replace the other. And you are going to learn to replace smoking with activity so there is no danger at all that you will start overeating. On the contrary, you'll be too busy to eat too much.

Using the advice in this book will make becoming a non-smoker interesting and easy to achieve, so all you have to do is follow the instructions all the way through and you'll have only good things to come with no stress, worry or negative feelings about failure, weight-gain or struggling to cope with the process of "giving up" a bad habit that you've spent years wishing you'd never started in the first place.

Chapter 3

Why Quitters Quit Quitting

There are more people who fail at giving up smoking than those who succeed.

The main reason is that most people who want to quit smoking are looking for that illusive "magic pill. " They're looking for something that will make them WANT to stop smoking. Sadly, there is no magic pill that can take away the desire to smoke. Wanting to quit has to be an individual choice. There is nothing that can do this for you. Becoming a non-smoker has to be your number one goal and you have to feel good about it.

And that is the hardest part of giving up smoking. You really have to want to do it.

This book WILL teach you how to get cigarettes out of your life forever, but it has to be what you WANT to do and you have to be willing to learn. And as the saying goes, when the student is ready, the teacher will appear. For you, if you're really ready to stop smoking, and it's what you want to do, then this book is the teacher that you've been searching for.

But you MUST be sure that the thought of giving up cigarettes is something that you are looking forward to, and not something that you're secretly dreading. If the thought of not smoking any more distresses you in any way then you're really not ready to quit smoking because if you don't want to stop, you'll be opposed to quitting and you so you won't even try. You'll even attempt to fool yourself that you're going to stop smoking, but it won't work. You can't kid yourself.

Reading this book and thinking about the day when you finally put out a cigarette for the last time should fill you with happiness and give you a general all-over feeling of bliss. And once you have that feeling, nothing can stop you.

Becoming a non-smoker will not make you lonely for your cigarettes. You won't be bored without your cigarettes. Using the methods set out in this book will help you to keep active while you stop the smoking habit. And that doesn't mean that you'll be expected to go out and exercise. You'll just be moving on with the next thing you need to be doing instead of sitting around and pining for a cigarette all the time.

And because you won't be giving up all at once, the transition from smoker to non-smoker will be so smooth that you'll hardly notice it happening at all.

And you mustn't worry yourself about what other smokers think about you while you're quitting. They'll hate the fact that you're doing it because they will be pea-green with envy. Their jealousy may even make them vocal with jibes about how you'll fail. But just ignore it all.

You may even get snide comments from non-smokers who'll smirk and say "Yeah, sure you're going to quit. Just like all the others who tried and failed. " But just ignore them too. They've simply seen so many smokers fail to quit that they don't believe that you'll succeed. And also, to a non-smoker, the subject of smoking (or quitting) is boring because they really don't care whether you smoke or not.

But if you're ready to quit and you're really looking forward to doing it, then nothing will get you down and you won't care what anyone says, which is how it should be.

There are two reasons why smokers fail to quit but neither of them will apply to you if you give up smoking by following all the steps in this book.

Firstly, smokers fail to quit because the temptation to smoke is too great when they go "cold turkey. " They just go through the day wishing more than anything that they could have a cigarette. Soon they find themselves thinking about smoking so much that they just go ahead and light one up because smoking is easier than not smoking when it's what they really want to do. They convince themselves that "just one cigarette" won't hurt.

The second reason is because they forget they're giving up if they're trying to do it slowly. It's easy to try and "cut down" by designating certain times of the day to smoke or deciding not to have a cigarette at certain times. But doing it this way is just another way of suffering from cigarette deprivation. That's why doing it by using this book is so much better because you won't have to stop smoking by using either of those methods.

You also won't be spending your time envying other smokers because the methods used in this book allow you to carry on smoking while, at the same time, changing your smoking habits until smoking is no longer a habit at all.

You won't suffer from wishing you could smoke but not being able to. You won't have to worry about whether this method of giving up smoking will work or not because it will be working the whole time you're doing it and you won't even notice that you're quitting.

So what will you be doing? And what makes this method so easy?

Let's discuss it in the next chapter.

Chapter 4

Why It's Hard to Quit and What to Do About It

There's no doubt about it. As soon as you stop smoking, you immediately want another cigarette. Usually you can go two or three hours without a cigarette. But if you quit smoking suddenly, 5 minutes without a cigarette seems like a very long time. Not only that, but the rest of your life seems like a scarily long time to not have a cigarette.

No wonder it's so hard to stop smoking this way. No one wants to spend every day of the rest of their life wanting something they can't have, no matter what it is. So if you spend every day of your life longing for a cigarette, eventually that longing will turn into resentment. And in the end you'll start smoking again because even though you want to stop, the guilt you feel from smoking is easier to bear than the constant feelings of resentment.

It's also easy to convince yourself that smoking cigarettes has therapeutic value. Just like a junkie taking a fix, you feel less anxious every time you smoke and so cigarettes appear to be a stress reliever. But the only anxiety you were feeling was your desire to smoke, so once you lit a cigarette your anxiety diminished.

But that doesn't mean that smoking cigarettes can relieve anxiety about other things. On the contrary; it can make you feel even more anxious. Even on TV shows you can see worried people light up a cigarette and then put it out a few seconds later because it didn't calm them down. Instead it just seemed to make them more nervous.

Giving up smoking can also make you eat more. Because smoking is an oral fixation, it may seem tempting to replace putting cigarettes in your mouth with putting food in your mouth instead. But this will only leave you feeling dissatisfied because food won't give you the cigarette "fix" you're craving. And when you start to gain weight you'll start to smoke again because cigarettes will seem like the lesser evil compared to food.

And if you mix into this the emotional loss from parting with your dear, sweet constant companions called cigarettes, it's no wonder giving them up seems so hard.

So having said all this, how exactly are you going to stop smoking AND find it easy to do?

Well, as the title of this books says, you're going to quit without giving up cigarettes. Now that may sound impossible but it's not. And that's what makes this method of quitting so easy to do.

If I told you to stop smoking in any way, even something simple like don't have a cigarette after a meal any more then straight away you'd feel like you were going to be deprived of your smoking enjoyment. And that's why I'm not going to tell you to do that. I'm not going to deprive you of any of the cigarettes you want to smoke.

Does that sound intriguing? Well you'll soon find out how you're going to do it.

This book is a complete course in becoming a non-smoker and if you follow every step of the process, you'll be a non-smoker 9 months from now.

And because you'll have done it step-by-step and day-by-day, you'll be a non-smoker for the rest of your life. Guaranteed. You'll finally feel strong and more in control of your life once you've conquered the constant, unwanted and unwelcome urge to smoke.

And because you don't have to quit smoking all at once, or try to quit on your own without any help, or buy any expensive stop-smoking products, you'll find the whole experience of cutting cigarettes out of your life easy and even enjoyable.

It isn't difficult to quit when you know how to do it and you're given guidance every step of the way.

But as previously mentioned, you MUST be in the right frame of mind to quit before you begin.

So first of all I need to ask, "Are You Ready To Become A Non-Smoker?"

Chapter 5

The Right Frame of Mind For Quitting

Let me ask you a very important question:

Do you want to stop smoking?

The answer to that has to be yes, you do want to stop smoking. Don't confuse this with thinking that you want something that will MAKE you want to stop smoking.

Miracle cures don't exist, but the will to stop smoking does.

So you need to understand that you must be ready to MAKE yourself stop smoking. And the thought of being a non-smoker MUST be a happy thought and not one that fills you with dread.

I know that I've already labored on this point a lot, but it really is THE most important part of becoming a non-smoker, because if you really don't want to stop smoking then nothing in the whole world will make you stop. Even if you've convinced yourself that using this book will make you stop even if you don't want to, you're kidding yourself.

You might even still carry on reading and start following all the advice. But you'll soon get bored with it because it's not what you really want to do. You might also get worried when it starts working because you don't really want to succeed in becoming a non-smoker.

Either way you'll start cheating and then you'll blame the methods in this book and say, "that didn't work!" But it would have if you'd done it. But if you don't want to be a non-smoker you won't follow the methods through the whole nine months.

And so you'll just tell yourself that you simply CAN'T stop smoking, when it would be more truthful to say that you WON'T.

But you can only stop smoking if you're quitting for the right reasons.

When I was a smoker and I was trying different ways to stop, most of the material I read talked a lot about the health issues attached to smoking. But although I was smoking 20 or more cigarettes a day, I never felt unhealthy or out of breath. I was actually slim, active and never felt better so being told that it was ruining my health did nothing towards making me want to stop.

I was once in hospital with a punctured lung and the doctor warned me not to move around too much and definitely not to smoke.

The next day a man in a wheel chair was brought into the same ward. He too had a punctured lung and his breathing seemed labored. Later that day I went into the Day Room to get a magazine to read. The man in the wheelchair was there smoking a cigarette (smoking was allowed in the Day Room back then). His wife was with him and when she saw the shocked look on my face when I saw the cigarette, she smiled sheepishly and said, "He just loves smoking. "

That's why there isn't much mentioned about health issues in this book. If you're a smoker, you don't care about your health otherwise you wouldn't be smoking. So telling you that smoking is ruining your health won't make any difference to you because you already know that and you don't care.

Everyone has their personal reasons for quitting but they have to be your own reasons and no one else's. For instance, giving up smoking "for the sake of the children" won't work. Giving up because of "anti-smoking social pressure" won't work either.

You have to want to stop smoking because you want to become a non-smoker and not because you think other people want you to.

Your desire to be a non-smoker must be stronger than your desire to smoke. Every time you think about your future life as a non-smoker it should excite you.

You need to be envious of people who don't smoke and want to be just like them.

Once you become a non-smoker you'll start hating cigarettes. Every time you go shopping and you see cigarette packets on the shelves you may even feel angry at them because you were once forced to buy them all the time.

And of course, once you stop smoking for good you'll get negative pressure from people who still smoke, especially those you used to smoke with.

The problem though is that once you no longer smoke, being around people who do smoke will be difficult; not because you'll want to smoke too, but because you'll realize how bad cigarettes smell and you won't want to inhale the smoke any more, even if it's second-hand smoke from other people's cigarettes.

Naturally your old smoking buddies will see this as some kind of snobbery when you don't want to be around them when they're smoking. But that's OK. It's their problem, not yours. As long as you're determined to be a non-smoker for the rest of your life and it's something that you want more than anything else, then nothing will stand in your way.

But you need to realise, if you haven't already, that becoming a non-smoker is a very solitary journey to take. No one can help you. No one will want to know how you're doing.

Can you handle this alone?

Yes you can.

So now it's time to get started. It's time to take the first step on the road to becoming a non-smoker.

Using this book is easy.

The following chapters each contain your instructions for one month. So the next chapter (chapter 6) contains your instructions for the first month.

So read the following chapter and then follow the instructions for one whole month before reading the next chapter.

Then continue through the rest of the book in the same way. Read one chapter at a time and follow the all the advice for one whole month before you read the next chapter.

So now that you're ready, we'll begin...

Chapter 6

Becoming a Non-Smoker

Month One

The biggest problem with smoking is that it's a habit that is ingrained in your daily life and has been for a long time.

No doubt you've often wanted to break this habit but the only way you could think to do it was by stopping either gradually or all at once. But as you've probably already discovered, neither of these ways is very successful.

So now you are going to try something different.

When you smoke cigarettes throughout the day, you tend to time them with certain events such as after a meal or with a cup of coffee (or a cup of tea). So what you need to do is slightly alter the times that you smoke.

This first step is only a small one and you may feel that it's hardly worth doing. But because it's the first step it's also the most important. So don't feel as though it's a waste of time because it isn't. Remember that this is a slow method of giving up smoking and it's also, and most importantly, a permanent method of giving up.

So take this first small, and important, step and do it for a whole month. It might make it easier if you begin on the first day of the month so that you won't forget when your month is up.

And although this first step is simple, don't rush it and try to get onto the next month too soon. And don't cheat. Never, ever cheat. Just follow this rule for one whole calendar month – without cheating – and then move onto the next step.

The First Step

So right now this very minute is when you're going to start becoming a non-smoker. And when I say right now, I mean RIGHT NOW; not later, not tomorrow or next week. Right now.

From this moment on, until the end of the month, (or until this date next month) you are going to use the 15 Minute Rule.

This rule is simple.

All you have to do is wait 15 minutes after eating or after a cup of tea or coffee before you smoke a cigarette.

Normally you probably light up a cigarette as soon as you finish eating or you smoke while you're having a cup of tea or coffee. But now your routine has changed and you must wait 15 minutes.

And you must not sit around doing nothing while you wait. If you've just finished dinner you can clear the table and rinse the dishes. If you've just had a snack or a cup of coffee, then go back to whatever you were doing before and then take a cigarette break in 15 minutes.

If you're at work and your coffee break isn't long enough for you to be able to wait 15 minutes, then smoke your cigarette BEFORE you drink your coffee. You must NOT take even one sip of coffee while you're smoking. Just leave the cup on the table and don't pick it up till you've extinguished your cigarette.

And it's not just tea or coffee that you need to apply the 15 Minute Rule to. It applies to any drink, even a glass of milk, a glass of water or a soft drink. So remember when the rule says "coffee" it really applies to any drink or beverage.

The 15 Minute Rule also applies to getting up and going to bed. You must not smoke a cigarette within 15 minutes of getting up. Likewise, you cannot have a cigarette during the last 15 minutes before you go to bed.

If you're a person who smokes in bed before you actually get up in the morning, then please note that the terms "getting up" and "waking up" mean the same thing. You must get out of bed every morning as soon as you wake up. No more laying there for ages thinking about getting up but not actually doing anything about it. So the sooner you get out of bed every morning, the sooner you can have your first cigarette of the day, once you've waited for 15 minutes.

And if you usually smoke in bed at night, then that's a habit that you're going to have to break because it's so dangerous that you really should never do it and any sensible adult would never want to do it anyway. Smoking in bed when you're tired is quite simply a stupid thing to do. So from now on your bedroom will be a smoke-free zone.

Just spend the next month integrating the 15 Minute Rule into your life. It's such a simple rule that you shouldn't find it difficult to do at all.

However, there's just one more thing...

While you're smoking, you mustn't be doing anything else at the same time. Just sit (or stand) and smoke your cigarette. Be aware of every inhale and every exhale and really make sure that you know you're smoking so that you enjoy every second. Don't watch TV while you smoke or read a magazine or check your emails or send a text message or anything else.

Just wait for 15 minutes after eating or after a cup of tea or coffee or upon rising or going to bed. Keep busy and active during your 15 minute wait and then relax and enjoy your cigarette without being interrupted or distracted.

And remember...no cheating. Make sure you wait the full 15 minutes every time. Don't try and wait longer and definitely don't wait less than 15 minutes. And never chain smoke because that's cheating too.

The 15 Minute Rule also applies to the waiting time in between cigarettes. This doesn't mean that you have to light up a cigarette every 15 minutes, but rather you must wait at least 15 minutes after smoking one cigarette before you can have another.

So that's it for this month. Just use the 15 Minute Rule and we'll continue on the journey next month in Chapter 7.

P. S. Each month only buy your cigarettes one packet at a time. Don't stockpile them. You'll see why as we go along.

Chapter 7

Becoming a Non-Smoker

Month Two

By now you should be very used to the 15 Minute Rule and it should already be such an ingrained part of your daily life that you do it without thinking about it.

They say that if you do something consistently for 30 days it becomes a habit, even if it's something that you find hard to do like going to the gym or losing weight.

But even though you now find the 15 Minute Rule easy to do, you still need to stay focused on your goal. It would be very simple now for you to feel that you've somehow succeeded in what you're trying to achieve and this would make you complacent.

So although coming this far is a successful step, it's still only one step and so you need to keep going and take the next step.

The Second Step

Now that you've conquered the 15 Minute Rule, it's now time to extend it into the 30 Minute Rule.

This new rule works in exactly the same way as the 15 Minute Rule except that you now have to wait an extra 15 minutes. But that will be so easy to do because you're already used to waiting 15 minutes.

Also don't forget that you can't smoke within the last 30 minutes before you go to bed and you must now also wait a minimum of 30 minutes between cigarettes.

If you've been having your first cigarette of the day 15 minutes after you get out of bed, you're now going to change this routine completely.

From now on you can't have your first cigarette of the day until after breakfast, even if your breakfast is only a cup of coffee.

AND...remember you must now wait 30 minutes after a meal or drink before you can have a cigarette.

And there is also one more small change you're going to make to your smoking habit.

Imagine that you have gone to the shop to buy a packet of cigarettes but they have sold out of your usual brand. What brand would you buy instead? What is your second favorite brand of cigarettes?

Well this month you are only going to buy your second favorite brand of cigarettes. But don't worry because it won't be as bad as you think. It may not be your preferred choice, but your second favorite brand is still one of your favorites, right?

You should also refrain from smoking other people's cigarettes. You need to stick to the brand you're smoking. And even if someone is smoking the same brand, smoking theirs can lead to you over-smoking because you'll forget how many cigarettes you've had. And because they're not sticking to the 30 Minute Rule, they could influence you to break the rule yourself and after coming this far it would be a shame to let someone else undo all your good work.

Just stick to smoking your own cigarettes and stay strong, focused and in control of what you're doing.

Go out now and buy your second favorite brand of cigarettes and start using the new 30 Minute Rule.

And next month I'll teach you several new things that can really help you on your journey to becoming a non-smoker.

Chapter 8

Other Things You Must Do Now

Month Three

By now you should be finding it really easy to use the 30 Minute Rule and you should be quite used to smoking your second favorite brand of cigarettes. If you are then congratulations on being controlled and focused enough to do it, and keep it up for another month.

If you've found the last month to be a struggle then toughen up soldier and stop feeling so sorry for yourself.

This month you're going to continue to use the 30 Minute Rule.

But this isn't all you'll be doing, because now I'm going to give you six new strategies to add to your non-smoking arsenal. These are six things that you must start doing straight away and keep on doing them until you become a non-smoker.

Make sure you do them consistently without any whinging, whining or cheating. It may seem like a lot to do all at once but it isn't. And what's more, you should find it fun.

Shop Around

You're probably like every other person who smokes when it comes to buying cigarettes. You probably buy them from the same shop every time. Well now you're no longer going to buy your cigarettes there. Instead you're going to buy your cigarettes from the next place you'd go to if your usual shop didn't exist.

Just pretend that the usual shop you buy your cigarettes from no longer exists or no longer sells cigarettes. Where would you buy them from instead?

Just make sure the shop you choose is not in the same shopping mall as your usual shop or not in the same street.

Once you know where you're going to buy them from this is now your usual place where you'll buy your cigarettes from and you can never go back to your 'old' place again.

And remember, you're now only buying your cigarettes one packet at a time. No stockpiling allowed.

Move Your Cigarettes

Don't keep your cigarettes in the same place any more. You probably have a place where you keep your open packet of cigarettes. Maybe you keep them in your pocket, or on the coffee table or in the kitchen draw. But now it's time to keep them elsewhere.

You can keep them anywhere you choose but it must be a place that makes you move further to get them.

For instance, you can keep them on the top shelf of the closet in your spare bedroom, or in the bathroom, in the garage or in the shed at the bottom of the garden. But wherever you choose, make sure it's somewhere that takes a bit of effort for you to get to them.

And then every week move them to a new place, but make sure it still takes effort to get to them.

No More Indoor Coziness

From now on you can only smoke outside. No matter how bad the weather is you must go outside to smoke (preferably somewhere covered if it's raining).

It doesn't matter if you're at home or some place where there is a designated smoking area. You must still go outside if you want a cigarette.

No More Social Smoking

You must always smoke alone. If that's not possible (if you're at work and everyone goes out at the same time) then you mustn't talk, or at least keep talking to a minimum.

While you're smoking, that must be the only thing you're doing. Keep looking at the cigarette the whole time it's between your fingers. Keep your focus on it from the moment you pick it up to the moment you put it out.

Get a Butt Jar

Find a large, empty glass jar. Fill it with about an inch of water. Whenever you smoke a cigarette, throw the butt into your butt jar, close the lid, give it a shake and then open it and take a sniff of the contents.

Keep on adding your butts to it every day and add more water if it runs low and the butts start to dry up.

Continue shaking and sniffing the jar after each butt is added.

Cut Out Other Sneaky Smoking Habits

There are times when you habitually smoke without thinking about it and so far these have not been mentioned. But now you need to tackle them.

For instance, you may be in the habit of lighting up a cigarette every time you get in the car or when you're talking on the telephone. But you're not going to do this any longer.

From now on you'll wait till you're out of the car or off the telephone before you light up a cigarette, provided, of course, that it's more than 30 minutes since your last one.

And remember that in the car and talking on the phone are only examples. There might be other triggers that make you automatically light up a cigarette that you need to address.

Just make sure that every time you're smoking, that's all you're doing, and you won't go wrong.

And you may think that you have a lot of new habits to get into this month, but each of them is simple and easy to do. And with so many new ideas to implement, it will keep you busy and alert for the next calendar month.

But before you begin, I'd like you to read the next chapter first.

Chapter 9

Alcohol and Smoking

Drinking alcohol is always a problem for anyone trying to quit smoking so this subject needs a chapter all of its own.

The trouble with alcohol is that every time you have a drink it seems like a great idea to have another...and another...and another. So this causes two separate problems.

First of all your mouth seems so wet after a drink that you'll be dying to smoke a cigarette to dry it up.

Secondly, after a few more drinks your judgment will be so impaired from all the alcohol that you won't know if you're smoking or not. And it's these two problems that can really stumble you when you're trying to quit. So this is why alcohol needs to be brought into the smoking rules.

So if you're going to drink alcohol during the next few months, I'll tell you how to incorporate it into your new monthly regime.

First you must still carry on with what you've been doing so far. This means you cannot smoke within 30 minutes of having a drink and you must also wait 30 minutes between cigarettes.

But the rules slightly change with alcohol.

Say you drink a glass of beer. You will then have to wait 30 minutes before you can have a cigarette. Normally this would mean that you can't have another drink for 30 minutes either, otherwise you'd have to start your 30-minute wait from the time you finish your second drink.

In a social setting where alcohol is flowing, it's not always possible to wait 30 minutes between drinks, whether they are alcoholic or not.

So when it comes to alcohol, the rule is as follows:

After you finish your first drink, you must wait 30 minutes before you can have a cigarette. Naturally, you'll want to have another drink during this time without having to start your 30-minute wait all over again.

So wait your 30 minutes after your first drink. If you want to have another drink that's fine. When at least 30 minutes is up after your first drink you can have a cigarette. But you can't smoke it while drinking another drink. This will mean that you'll have to wait until after you've finished your second drink, and smoke your cigarette before you get your third drink.

And social smoking still isn't allowed. You must go outside to smoke and try not to talk to anyone. Just focus on your cigarette until it's finished and then you can go back inside.

If you're at a social gathering that's already in an outdoor setting, say at barbeque in someone's backyard or a night-time party on a beach, you must still go away from everyone else to smoke your cigarette.

If you then go back to the party and have another drink, you'll have to wait a minimum of 30 minutes after you finish it and you mustn't smoke while you're having your next drink.

Just keep on doing this throughout the evening and you may even find that you drink less (which is always a good thing) because your mouth won't be as dry from smoking as it normally is and so your thirst won't be as great.

Another problem with these types of social situations is the pressure you might get from other smokers. When they see that you're not smoking while you're drinking, they will probably try and taunt you into changing your mind.

Be firm with them and explain that smoking while you're drinking isn't something that you want to do any more. And once they see how strong you are about your convictions, they should leave you alone.

Remember that other people who smoke don't want you to stop smoking. They want you to fail so that they can sneer and say "I told you so. " But this time you've already come so far and achieved so much that their opinion won't matter to you anymore.

And if, for any reason, you do find yourself back-sliding and smoking when you shouldn't, don't punish yourself over it. Just get straight back on track and keep going.

But I know that you won't back-slide because if you've come this far, you're too strong to give up now.

Chapter 10

Becoming a Non-Smoker

Month Four

Welcome to your fourth month of becoming a non-smoker, and congratulations for making it this far.

By now you must be feeling incredibly pleased with yourself. You should also be able to notice a slight reduction in the number of cigarettes you smoke, which has come about because of the changes you've made to your smoking habit.

And the best thing about it is that changing your smoking habit was so easy that you hardly noticed you were doing it. But you must continue with the 30 Minute Rule and you MUST keep busy during the 30 minutes after eating and drinking. As long as you stay occupied while you wait, then the 30 Minute Rule will be easy to do.

This month I want you to check your weight. It's important to check it to make sure you're not using food to compensate yourself for not smoking. Be sure that you're not putting extra food on your plate at meal times and don't eat any more snacks than you used to do.

And definitely (and this is extremely important) don't eat anything while you're waiting 30 minutes till your next cigarette. Make sure you don't start fooling yourself by thinking that it's OK to eat straight after a meal, because if you do, you'll have to wait 30 minutes after you've finished your snack before you can have a cigarette.

And that is not how the 30 Minute Rule works.

Eating straight after a meal is just the same as replacing a cigarette with food, and that is something you must never do.

If you eat straight after a meal, it means that you're not following the 30 Minute Rule. It's as though you just feel you need SOMETHING straight after a meal, and if a cigarette isn't available, you simply replace it with a desert or a snack food, and tell yourself it's OK because you'll time your 30 minutes from when you've finished eating.

But it's not OK. It's not OK at all. You need to eat your normal meal and then wait the 30 minutes from when you finish. The whole idea of the 30 Minute Rule is so that you get used to not having anything after a meal. You can't have a snack, or a sugary treat of any kind - not even a piece of chewing gum.

Just keep busy for 30 minutes without eating, chewing, drinking or inhaling anything. In other words, nil-by-mouth.

And if you're doing everything right you'll be smoking less and not gaining weight.

Just follow all the previous rules about smoking outside, smoking alone, changing where you keep your cigarettes every week, using your butt jar and, of course, being constantly and continually faithful to the 30 Minute Rule.

Over the last couple of months you also changed to your second favorite brand of cigarettes and started buying them from a different shop. And now I want you to change these two things again.

First you have to think of what your third favorite brand of cigarettes is. At the moment you're smoking your second favorite. But what if they were no longer available either? What would your next choice be? Whatever brand it is, this is now the brand you'll be smoking this month.

But don't go and buy them from the shop that you're now normally buying your cigarettes from. You've already changed from where you originally bought your cigarettes from to a shop further away. Now you have to pretend that neither of those places exists anymore and you now have to find a third alternative place to buy our cigarettes.

And just as before, it can't be in the same shopping mall or the same street as where you were previously buying them from.

And you must still only buy your cigarettes one packet at a time. Even if you think you're too busy to go out buying cigarettes several times a week, do it anyway. No excuses. Even if it means going out at night or getting up earlier in the morning. Do it. Just fit your new cigarette regime into your life and do it.

By now you should be very comfortable in your new way of smoking. Waiting 30 minutes should be simple and using your butt jar should be an automatic habit.

So now it's time to kick back, relax and enjoy the new way that you approach smoking, safe in the knowledge that in a few weeks' time you'll be a non-smoker for life.

And won't that be great?

See you next month.

Chapter 11

A Few More Extras

Month Five

Now that you're four months into this new way of smoking, you should be able to notice quite a few changes in yourself.

Firstly your breath must have improved now that you're not smoking as many cigarettes. And consequently you'll probably notice that your food tastes stronger. That's because nicotine has a really damaging effect on your taste buds and really dulls your sense of taste. So as your taste buds begin to recover, you'll notice the taste of your food getting stronger so you can really start enjoying your meals. And if smoking affected your breathing, then you've probably noticed a difference in this too.

And when it comes to money, smoking less can certainly make your richer. I don't think anyone is aware of the real financial cost of smoking until they stop. So after four months of smoking less, your purse/wallet must feel heavier than usual because of all the extra money that's in it.

So now that you're doing so well on your journey to becoming a non-smoker, it's time to try a few extra things that will help you along the way.

The first new thing you're going to try is a change in cigarettes. But unlike the last two times you don't have to change the place you buy them from and you may not even have to change brand.

What you are going to do this month is start smoking cigarettes with a lower tar content. All cigarettes produce tar and it's usually easy to spot the lower tar cigarettes because they're described on the packet as "low tar" or "light" or "mild. " If the brand of cigarettes you're currently smoking has a "light" option then buy those instead.

Some tobacco companies in some countries state the tar content on their cigarette packets. Here in Australia, where this book is published, stating tar content on cigarette packets is illegal as it's said to mislead people into believing that the cigarettes they're smoking are good for their health.

But if you live somewhere that allows tar content to be stated on the cigarette packets, then it will be easy to find a cigarette with lower tar content than the one you're currently smoking. For instance, if the tar content on your cigarettes is 16mg, then look for a brand that has a tar content of 10 or 12mg. but as before, make it a brand you don't usually smoke.

There may be a temporary draw back to smoking cigarettes with less tar, but just remember that it's only temporary. The drawback is that because you've been smoking for a long time, there could be a build up of sticky dark tar on your lungs.

But as you smoke less and start smoking cigarettes that produce less tar, you could find that the build up on your lungs begins to clear which, unfortunately, can result in you literally "coughing it up. " and although this cough may seem hard to deal with at first, just remember that it is only temporary and as soon as all the filth on your lungs clears, the coughing will stop. But if you're worried about it, then do consult your doctor, otherwise stick to your low tar cigarettes and let the coughing subside in its own time.

Another thing that you are going to change this month is the 30 Minute Rule. From now on it will be a 45 Minute Rule. The way this rule works is exactly the same as the 30 Minute Rule except that you'll be waiting 45 minutes instead.

You've been using the 30 Minute Rule for quite a number of weeks now, so changing the 30 minutes to 45 minutes will be simple.

One difference you will have noticed by now, and you'll notice even more with the 45 Minute Rule, is that you have a lot more spare time now.

Before you embarked on this journey to becoming a non-smoker, you probably sat down and smoked a cigarette immediately after every meal. The only problem with sitting down and relaxing in this way (apart from the poison you inhale) is that once you sit down, it's hard to get up again. It's all too easy to just stay where you are and light up another cigarette.

But now that you have to wait before you can smoke AND you have to stay active, you find that jobs you usually avoid doing (washing dishes, vacuuming carpets, cleaning the car, etc.) are now getting done during your waiting times.

And this leaves you with more free time to do the things you enjoy in your spare time. So now it's a really good time to start a new hobby or interest, or even take up an old hobby that you thought you didn't have time for any more.

For instance, is there a sport that you used to enjoy such as netball, tennis or martial arts? Or perhaps you've always wanted to learn how to knit, do upholstery or learn Japanese?

Well now that you're finding yourself with more free time - and you don't want to waste it on cigarettes - it's a great time to start doing something that you really enjoy.

Just give it some thought. You don't have to come up with an idea straight away, but just keep it in mind and soon something will come up. It may even be that you simply want to have more days out with your family, or you want to take a holiday or re-decorate your house. Just think of something that you REALLY want to do. Then make it happen.

This month is also the time to relax more. You have been trying really hard to follow all these rules and guidelines and now you need to take a bit of time out for some total - and I mean TOTAL - relaxation. Because not only do you deserve it, but it will help you to completely unwind and keep your mind in harmony with what you want to achieve, which is, of course, to become a non-smoker.

So I want you to buy a relaxation CD and listen to it for about 30 minutes a day. There are plenty of meditation CDs available and most of them will have sections of music and/or audio that lasts for about 30 to 45 minutes at a time. It should state this on the sales page or on the CD cover itself.

But any quality CD will do. Just transfer the sounds/music to your iPod or MP3 player (or download it straight from the internet) and then listen, relax and enjoy it every day.

If you can't find the time to listen to it every day, then listen to it as often as you can because relaxing this way really does have fantastic therapeutic value. And even if you're skeptical that this can help you, just try it for a month because I KNOW you'll benefit greatly from it.

And while you're laying (or sitting) and listening to your CD, think about how good you'll be feeling in a few weeks time when you no longer have to smoke. Just being free and knowing that you'll soon be unshackling yourself from the control that cigarettes have had over your life will be a feeling of exhilaration like you've never felt before.

So use your 30 minutes of quiet meditation time every day to think about and look forward to the day you can say goodbye to cigarettes for good.

And if there's anything else that will also calm your mind and help you break your cigarette "chains" (perhaps yoga, swimming, jogging?) then do that too. Anything that is in your arsenal and will help you win the tobacco war; do it! Start right now.

This month is also a good time to spring clean your house. Washing down every surface and cleaning out every cupboard and washing every carpet, curtain and upholstered piece of furniture will help to eliminate all the tobacco-related smells from your home and therefore remove them from your mind.

Even if you think your house doesn't smell because you always smoke outside, don't kid yourself.

Cigarette smells can seep through windows, walls and doors. Even if you think the house is closed up while you're outside smoking, the smell will still find its way inside. It will also be clinging to you so when you finish your cigarette and walk back inside, the smell will go right in with you.

And while you're spring cleaning your house with soap and cleaning your mind with meditation, why not make it a really complete month by cleaning your body as well. And by that I don't mean the outside of your body.

This month would be the perfect time to detox your insides by cutting out (or at least cutting back) on junk food and alcohol.

Cutting down on alcohol is easy because while you're spring cleaning your house and listening to our meditation CDs, you won't have time to drink.

And to cut down on junk food, you need to stop eating fast food and only eat slow food. Slow food is the opposite to fast food. Fast food is highly processed junk that masquerades as food. Slow food is a meal that is prepared from only fresh ingredients. It contains nothing processed, tinned or dried. Organic food is best (especially vegetables picked fresh from the garden) but if this isn't available then just use store-bought fresh ingredients, and the fresher the better.

Just one month on a slow food diet will make you look and feel great.

And that's it for this month. Simply smoke a "lighter" cigarette, buy a relaxation CD, change your waiting time from 30 to 45 minutes and use the extra time to detox your home, your body and your mind.

And by this time next month, you'll feel fantastic.

Chapter 12

Becoming a Non-Smoker

Month Six

Congratulations on making it into the sixth month of this incredible journey.

Using your relaxation CDs, cleaning your house and detoxing your body will have made you feel even more excited to continue this journey right to the end.

Just keep on keeping your house fresh, aired and clean and keep on using your relaxation CDs. Doing these two things alone will make you feel great.

Your low tar cigarettes will also help you feel somewhat healthier than smoking the heavier tar cigarettes and, if you're still eating slow food instead of fast food then you'll be feeling better than you have done for years.

Just keep up the good work you've been doing so far. And don't, whatever you do, get lazy.
Don't start thinking that you can slack off and not use your CDs or go back to eating junk food.

Any backward step now, no matter how small, can send you heading in the wrong direction and before you know it, you'll be right back to where you started from and your 5 months of effort will be wasted.

You're already over halfway to becoming a non-smoker. So keep on looking forward with joy to the day you can stop smoking for good - and - unlike all the other times you've tried and failed; this time you'll be GLAD that you don't have to smoke anymore, so being a non-smoker will be a happy occasion and one that you'll want to celebrate.

But for now, let's get on with the next leg or your journey.

To begin with, you're now going to smoke cigarettes with an even lower tar content. If your cigarettes list the tar content on the packet then it will be easy to choose a lighter option.

If you're unsure, then just look for cigarettes that are called "extra mild" or "extra light. " You can ask the person who works in the cigarette shop to help you choose. They should know which are the lighter or milder cigarettes.

Don't cheat on this important step. Don't just choose cigarettes that are slightly lower in tar content than the ones you're currently smoking. Make sure the tar content is significantly lower.

At first these mild cigarettes may seem extremely different than what you are currently smoking. But you'll be amazed how quickly you get used to them. And remember the saying that you only have to do something for 30 days for it to become a habit. So by the end of the month you'll hardly notice the change at all.

So finish smoking the packet of cigarettes you've got and then go out and find something much milder.

And the next thing you're going to change this month is the 45 Minute Rule. From now on you're going to wait one hour after meals, after a drink and between cigarettes.

You've already been waiting 45 minutes for the past month so increasing this time by only 15 minutes will be a snip.

But remember; keep active during that one hour. Don't sit around waiting for the time to pass. There are always things you could be doing. You could mow the lawn, plant a vegetable garden, clean the car, do the ironing, clean out the kitchen cupboards, bake a cake, swim, jog, walk the dog, visit a friend, play games with your kids or any number of other things.

Waiting for an hour after a meal may be a problem in the mornings if you have to go to work and can't wait around for an hour after breakfast. If this happens then you have two options.

The first is to get up an hour earlier.

But if getting up earlier really doesn't appeal to you (but I don't know why it wouldn't because getting up early every day means you can accomplish so much more in a day) then you'll have to wait till you get to work.

You may be thinking that this means you'll be missing your after-breakfast cigarette. This can seem like it if, for instance, you usually smoke a cigarette after breakfast AND when you get to work, which will now mean that your after-breakfast cigarette and arriving-at-work cigarette are now one in the same.

But, let's face it; you're going to give up smoking altogether soon anyway, so smoking one less cigarette every day now really doesn't matter very much. Does it?"

If you're really serious and 100% determined to become a non-smoker then giving up your first morning cigarette won't bother you at all because it is just part of the overall journey and you were going to have to give it up sooner or later anyway. So it doesn't matter if it happens now. Right?

But on the other hand, if you really don't have any intention of becoming a non-smoker, then you won't give up your first cigarette of the morning no matter what.

So it's your decision.

If you're serious about what you're doing and you really do want to be a non-smoker, then smoking one less cigarette every morning won't be a problem. On the contrary, you'll think it's a brilliant idea.

Now as well as your lower tar cigarettes and your slightly longer waiting period, you're also going to change one more thing.

No doubt you brush your teeth at least twice a day - in the morning and in the evening. You might even be an OC person who also brushes after every meal.

Well from now on, whatever your teeth-cleaning regime might have been, you're going to alter it. You can continue brushing your teeth at your regular times. This doesn't have to change. But now you're also going to brush your teeth after every cigarette AND use mouth wash.

When you're at home this won't be a problem. But obviously it won't always be practical if you're at work. So if you're not able to brush your teeth at work, at least use the mouthwash if you can.

During a coffee break at work you may not have the time to do either, but at lunch time you definitely will (unless of course you're eating lunch in a café or restaurant). But now that you have to wait an hour after eating to have a cigarette, if you're at work on your lunch break, you'll probably smoke BEFORE you eat, in which case, you will have time to brush and rinse.

Make sure you brush your teeth and rinse with mouthwash after every cigarette whenever you can, which should be most of the time.

And don't be lazy about doing this.

I know that after waiting an hour before you can finally sit down and have a cigarette you might not feel like going to the bathroom to clean your teeth and rinse your mouth, but do it anyway. And do it every time.

This is a very important part of your journey and it will really help to keep the taste of the cigarettes you smoke out of your mouth.

Remember that when you're a non-smoker, your mouth will feel (and smell) much fresher so you need to start experiencing it now.

And having a really fresh mouth will make you feel better as well as giving you a sample of how great it's going to be to get rid of the stale smell and taste of cigarettes.

Feeling this now will really help to boost your enthusiasm for becoming a non-smoker.

But be warned: as you begin to rid yourself of the smell and taste of cigarettes, you'll become more aware of it on other people who smoke.

You'll get a whiff of cigarette smoke on their clothes every time they come near you. And as they lean close to talk to you, you'll notice how stale their breath is and how much it stinks.

Just remember that the reason they smell so bad is because they aren't as fortunate as you. They are still addicted to the smoking habit and they don't know how to break it. While you, on the other hand, are well on your way to breaking the habit and, in fact, you're nearly a non-smoker already and that is why smokers smell so bad to you now.

So rejoice and feel wonderful at how far you've come and how many steps you've achieved along the way.

And this is also the month to spoil yourself in appreciation of all your accomplishments.

By now you must have saved a lot of money because you've been smoking less. So use this money to treat yourself to something that you'd really enjoy. Perhaps there's a new outfit you'd like to have, or a restaurant meal, or a family day out, or a movie you want to see at the cinema.

Whatever it is, you can have it because you deserve it. And it won't cost you any more than you'd normally spend because you're using the money that you would have spent on cigarettes, so you should feel really good about spending it on something more enjoyable.

Just look at it this way. Ordinarily you would have spent the money on cigarettes which are what you didn't want but you had to have them even though you hated the smoking trap you were in.

But now you're spending the money on something that you do want and it's something that you can REALLY enjoy.

How great is that?

Now go on and enjoy this month.

Chapter 13

The End of Your Journey

Months Seven AND Eight

The next two months are going to be really exciting for you because they are going to bring you to the end of your journey.

You've been traveling along the road to becoming a non-smoker for six months now and so you'll be feeling very different towards smoking than you did during your first month.

Back then you felt as though smoking was something that you wanted to stop doing. By now you should be feeling as though it's something that you CAN stop doing.

Every month for the past six months you've been moving step-by-step towards breaking the smoking habit and now you're all but there.

You need to keep on doing everything you've been doing so far and not let your new habits slip.
Keep on using your butt jar, only smoke outside, move your cigarettes to a new place each week, keep your house

clean, use the One Hour Rule, brush your teeth and rinse your mouth after every cigarette, use your relaxation CDs and keep on looking forward to the day you can quit smoking for good and become a non-smoker.

If you feel as though you're just "not quite" ready to become a non-smoker don't worry. I don't want you to do it now even if you wanted to.

The journey isn't over yet. You've still got two more months to go so carry on with everything that you've been doing so far.

For the next two months there are only 2 small changes that you are going to make.

The first is that you are going to change the type of cigarettes you smoke. I want you to find out which are the mildest, lightest, lowest tar cigarette that you can buy. You can find this out by Googling it online, asking other people who smoke or going to the cigarette shop and asking the staff who work there. You may even find it helpful to use all 3 methods to make sure.

Once you find out which are the lightest, mildest, lowest tar cigarettes that you can buy, these are what you'll be smoking for the next 2 months. And as before, buy your cigarettes one packet at a time. Don't stockpile them and don't even THINK of buying 2 packs at once to save time. One pack only is the rule. And because you're smoking much less than you used to, you'll be surprised at how few packets you'll actually buy.

The next change that you're going to make for the next 2 months is, you've guessed it, the one hour wait. Only this time instead of increasing the time by 15 minutes, it will increase by 30 minutes. So now the One Hour Rule is now the One and a Half Hour Rule.

But this extra increase in time won't bother you because you've become so used to waiting an hour, so an extra 30 minutes doesn't mean anything.

And that's the only two changes that you have to make. Smoke the mildest cigarettes on the market and increase your waiting time to 1 ½ hours.

And remember that these new rules are for the next TWO months, by the end of which time, you'll be ready to stop smoking for good.

So look forward to this time with rapture and exuberance because this is what you've been waiting for and what you've been working towards for months now.

Over the next 2 months you'll feel your desire to smoke diminishing. You'll find that the hour and a half will fly by and sometimes when you look at the clock you'll see that hours have passed by unnoticed without you even thinking about having a cigarette.

And this will give you a calm and relaxed feeling because you'll know that being a non-smoker is finally close to becoming a reality.

Smoking will no longer be a priority in your mind. You won't be thinking about your next cigarette while you're still smoking another.

In fact, you'll begin to wonder how you ever got so addicted to smoking in the first place. And the fear you used to feel whenever you thought about giving up smoking will be gone, because now it's simply the next step in your journey and it's not feared at all any more. It's anticipated.

So what you need to be doing during the next 2 months is thinking of a celebration. You need to celebrate your success and organise a dinner, a party, a holiday or any other way you want to celebrate your amazing achievement of becoming a non-smoker.

So start thinking now about how you want to celebrate and then organise it to happen in 2 month's time.

This really is a time for celebration, happiness and positive recognition of how far you've come and what you've accomplished.

Naturally, there'll be the still-smoking nay-Sayers who'll try and tell you that it won't last or that you'll never do it.

But ignore them.

When people are jealous they can say really negative and hurtful things.

Just be glad that you're escaping the smoking addiction for good, and leave the smokers to wallow in their own self-pity while you get on with celebrating.

And I'll see you in 2 months' time.

Chapter 14

Congratulations! You've Done It!

Month Nine

Well, here you are.

It's been a long journey but finally you're here. You've arrived. You've made it.

You've come such a long way and made remarkable progress since you started becoming a non-smoker all those months ago.

Do you remember when you first began using the 15 Minute Rule? Doesn't that seem like a very long time ago?

And month after month, step-by-step you've moved along and progressed to where you are now.

And where are you?

You are about to become a non-smoker for the rest of your life. You are about to throw the rest of your cigarettes in the bin and you are going to feel great about it.

Cigarettes have kept you slave-bound to them long enough, and now you can unfetter yourself from them for good.

You no longer have to smoke.

You're free!

You've worked hard for your freedom and now it's yours. So stand up, go and get your cigarettes, take them to the rubbish bin and cheerfully throw them in.

That's it. You've done it. You're free.

Now you can bask in the self-satisfaction of your amazing achievement of becoming a non-smoker.

You can now enjoy the freedom of being able to say, "No thanks. I don't smoke" next and every time someone asks you if you want a cigarette.

But just be careful not to go around bragging about your accomplishment to people who still smoke.

Remember that no so long ago you were in the same trap that they are still stuck in. Do you remember how awful it felt to want to stop smoking but not knowing how to do it?

Well anyone who smokes is still stuck in that trap so don't brag to them about how you freed yourself. It will only make them feel worse and make them angry with you.

That's the big "bummer" about becoming a non-smoker. It's such a personal journey that you can't share it with anyone. Non-smokers don't care that you did it and people who smoke don't want to know about your success that they themselves wish they could have.

But don't let that spoil your fun. Just enjoy every minute of being a non-smoker. And when you see someone else smoking, just feel pity for them but don't say anything. Just enjoy your new found freedom.

And don't worry about back-sliding. That won't happen. At the beginning of this book we talked about how you have to WANT to be a non-smoker in order to become one, because it's impossible to work towards a goal if the outcome isn't something that you want to achieve.

So you began by wanting to become a non-smoker, you spent the best part of a year working towards becoming a non-smoker, and now you've achieved your goal. So after all that, why would you want to go back to where you started when that's not where you want to be?

You hear stories all the time about people who stopped smoking for years, only to succumb to the temptation of smoking again.

But this won't happen to you because those people never really wanted to become non-smokers. But you did. And now you are a non-smoker, so enjoy it.

It's a good idea to keep using your relaxation CDs for at least another month, just to help you stay at ease with the transition of smoker to non-smoker.

There will be those in your life who smoke and will delight in telling you that you'll "come round" or that you'll "give in" and want to start smoking again.

But what they don't understand (and you can secretly smirk at this) is that you haven't "given up" smoking. You've gained the freedom of being a non-smoker and so smoking is an addiction you no longer want or need.

From now on you're going to enjoy a life with better health, more wealth and more free time. But the best thing is going to be that wonderful, exhilarating feeling of freedom you'll get now that you're no longer a slave to cigarettes.

You're going to feel strong and successful now that you've regained control of your life. No one wants that insecure feeling that comes from having an addiction.

It's hard when you have a bad habit and you don't feel strong enough to break it.

But now you are strong because you've achieved it. You took back control of your life piece-by-piece and now you feel stronger than ever.
So now it's time to celebrate your strength and your freedom.

If you've planned a celebratory treat then it's time to go and indulge yourself.

You deserve it.

Now go and enjoy the rest of your cigarette-free life.

End

www.ingramcontent.com/pod-product-compliance
Lightning Source LLC
Chambersburg PA
CBHW050559300426
44112CB00013B/1996